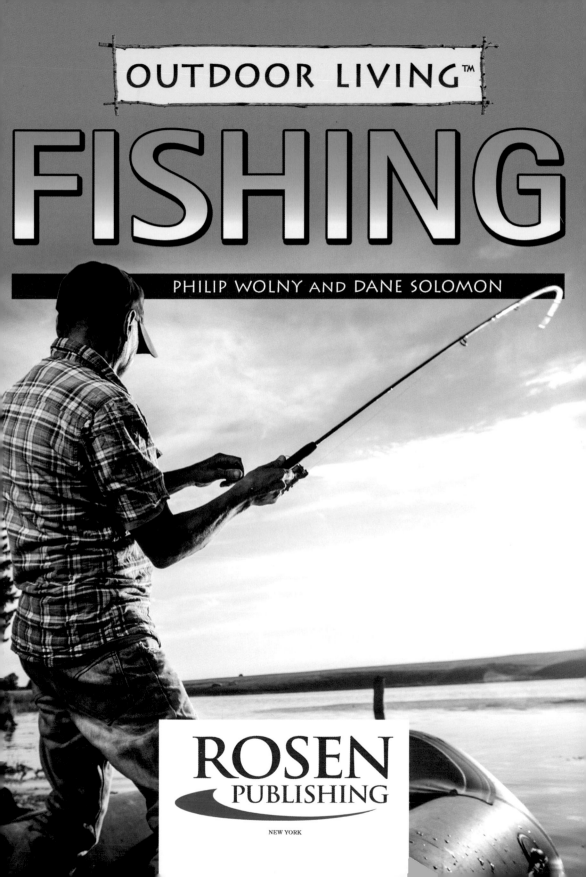

OUTDOOR LIVING™

FISHING

PHILIP WOLNY AND DANE SOLOMON

ROSEN
PUBLISHING

NEW YORK

Published in 2016 by The Rosen Publishing Group, Inc.
29 East 21st Street, New York, NY 10010

Copyright © 2016 by The Rosen Publishing Group, Inc.

First Edition

Library of Congress Cataloging-in-Publication Data

Wolny, Philip.
Fishing / by Philip Wolny and Dane Solomon p. cm. — (Outdoor living)
Includes bibliographical references and index.
ISBN 978-1-4994-6225-8 (library binding)
1. Fishing — Juvenile literature. I. Philip Wolny Solomon, Dane. II. Solomon,
Dane III. Title.
SH445.S68 2016
799.1—d23

Manufactured inChina

CONTENTS

INTRODUCTION

For thousands of years, human beings have fished. Early humans fished for survival, especially those living near water. In modern times, most people fish for enjoyment, while others fish to earn a living, and others do it as a professional sport. Some still fish to feed themselves, of course, and one benefit of good afternoon fishing is dining on what you have caught.

Anybody can fish, and people of all kinds and ages and abilities enjoy fishing worldwide. A person does not need to be born with special athletic talents, be a genius, or have a wrestler's physique to be a good fisherman. In addition, fishing does not require having to spend a lot of money on expensive equipment. Just going out and doing it may be as easy as getting to the closest creek, river, lake, or ocean shore near you.

If you are new to fishing and would like to know more about the sport, this book will give you an idea of how to get started. Beginners will get a good overview of different kinds of fishing they may want to try, while those who have fished already will benefit from the refresher course.

As with any physical activity, putting safety first is one of the most important rules when fishing. This is especially true due to the equipment used and because the sport happens on or next to water.

Fishing is enjoyed everywhere, and there is no time like the present to learn, so let's get started!

Burmese fishermen steer and paddle their boats with one foot and balance on the other, leaving their hands free for their fishing nets. This is a very ancient form of fishing.

CHAPTER 1

FISHING BASICS AND SAFETY

W hile modern equipment is different, fishing itself has not changed much in thousands of years. Many new tools are available to modern fishers. Beginners should note, however, that the main differences are in the materials and equipment used these days. Fishing tackle, including rods, reels, hooks, fishing line, and other tools like spears and nets, are made of different materials today. But the basic steps involved in catching fish have changed very little.

ANCIENT AND MODERN FISHING TOOLS

In the past, spears—primarily made of a sharpened piece of wood or bone attached to the end of a pole of some sort—were used to catch fish in shallow waters such as ponds, rivers, and streams.

A fisherman on the Shire River in southern Malawi casts his net. This traditional method, common in Africa and elsewhere, differs greatly from the means most Westerners employ.

Nets, made from woven materials such as thread or thin vines, and fish traps were used to catch large numbers of ocean fish.

Hook and line, a method very popular today, was used by people thousands of years ago as well. Hooks were made of shaped bone or wood, and fishing line was made from animal intestines or hair or from thin plant materials such as roots, vines, or certain types of grass.

Modern spears are made of stronger materials, such as aluminum or hard plastic. Nets are still woven, but they are woven with stronger, lighter materials. Fishing hooks are made from strong metals, such as steel or bronze, and fishing line is made from a material called monofilament.

FISH: HOW THEY MOVE

Anyone who has been swimming has found out that it is much harder to move your body through water than through air. This is because water is denser than air and gives more resistance.

Have you ever wondered how fish seem to move so quickly and gracefully? For starters, their streamlined shape lets fish glide through the water with a minimum of resistance. Fish also secrete a special kind of slime from their skin that helps them travel more smoothly through the water. By contrast, humans—having neither a streamlined shape nor special secretions for swimming—are at a great disadvantage when it comes to swimming.

As a fish swims, it relies on its skeleton for its framework, its muscles for power, and its fins for thrust and direction.

CLASSIFYING FISH

What do you think of when you think of fish? Fish are cold-blooded, meaning their body temperature is determined by their environment. They have fins, they have backbones, and they are classified as vertebrates, like reptiles, amphibians, and mammals. Fish have scales and breathe by passing water through their gills.

There are three classes of modern-day fish. Agnatha are primitive jawless fish like lampreys and hagfish. Chondrichthyes are jawed fish with skeletons made of cartilage and include creatures such as sharks and rays. The third are Osteichthyes, fish with bony skeletons, like trout, bass, and salmon.

FISHING TODAY

Fishing today can be divided into commercial and sport fishing. Most commercial fishing is done on a large scale, with fishing boats catching thousands of fish with nets, traps, hooks, and line. These fish are sold to distributors and make their way to restaurants and stores.

Sport fishing is a sport, pastime, and tradition. Much of it is done in rural areas, but many people in cities also fish, either nearby or during outings and vacations. Sport fishermen do not fish for commercial reasons, but for enjoyment. They enjoy the skill, concentration, and know-how involved. Many fish to relax and spend time outdoors. Going out with members of their family and/or friends is a great way to bond and embrace and appreciate nature. Catching your own supper is a bonus of fishing, too, and something to take pride in.

There are different kinds of fishing, depending on the location and equipment used. You can fish on lakes, streams, rivers, and other freshwater bodies of water, or in bays, in inlets, or on the ocean as a saltwater fisher. Different techniques and equipment work for different kinds of fish. The variety of combinations out there that make up the entire sport of fishing would not fit in a dozen books. But the following chapters will give you a basic breakdown of what to expect.

SAFETY—ABOVE ALL

Wherever you choose to fish, the number one rule is safety first, before anything else. Even fishing on man-made structures over or next to the water demands caution. Being safe is even more crucial out on the water. Whether you go out on a party boat to fish or take a small wooden rowboat into the middle of a lake, being careless can be fatal. There are things you can do before fishing—with a safety check—as well as being mindful while fishing.

Your safety check should include ensuring you have the following items: a life preserver or lifejacket for every person on board the boat; a noise-making device like a whistle or horn; a flare gun with flares; and a first-aid kit.

Wear your lifejacket at all times while on board. Avoid standing up when the boat is in motion. You could fall off if the boat hits a wave. Also make sure that all of the equipment you bring on the boat is stored safely so that it won't fall overboard or slide all over the boat and trip or injure someone.

SECURING GEAR

Handling fishing gear safely is important, too. Fishing hooks can be very dangerous if not handled properly. Always handle fishing hooks by the shank of the hook. Otherwise, you risk getting the point of the hook caught in your hand or some other part of your body. If you

Safety tips are often passed from one generation of fishermen to the next. An older, experienced angler, like one's grandfather, can provide invaluable advice to a beginner.

have had the misfortune of it happening to you, you know it is not a pleasant experience.

When storing hooks in your tackle box or on your fishing rod, remember to put a small cork or a piece of foam on the point. If you happen to grab the fishing rod or put your hand in the tackle box without looking, you will not get a hook stuck in your flesh.

FISHING

Always handle and store fishing knives cautiously. Remember to hold the knife by its handle, not by its blade. When you put it away, always put the knife into a protective holder to avoid hurting yourself or damaging anything you may have in your tackle box. Consult a parent or adult about how to use a fishing knife before handling it.

Fishing line can also be very dangerous when handled incorrectly. If you get tangled in line, you can cut yourself or even stop the blood flow from one part of your body to another. Ask a tackle shop employee or experienced fisherman for proper instruction on handling line.

CHAPTER 2

GEARING UP

Before heading to the pier or going out on the water, every beginning fisherman should become familiar with and obtain (or borrow or rent) at least some of the equipment he or she will need.

FISHING RODS

The first thing you need is a fishing rod. Besides homemade rods, made from wood or bamboo, most rods you will use will be store-bought.

Modern rods are made of either fiberglass or graphite. These materials provide a very delicate feel and the strength needed to bring fish of all sizes. They come in many sizes, and they range in price from two or three dollars to hundreds of dollars, depending on their quality and workmanship. A fishing rod consists of grips,

A close-up of someone holding a rod and reel. The guides on this spinning rod are on the underside of it.

a reel seat (where the fishing reel is placed on the rod), and fishing guides for the fishing line to go through.

There are two types of fishing rods. One type is a spinning fishing rod, which has extra big guides for the fishing line to go through. The guides are sized in such a way so that the line can pass through the guides with very little resistance when casting. The other type of fishing rod is the conventional fishing rod. These rods are used mostly when fishing from a boat, so they are sometimes called boat rods. This rod has smaller guides to keep the fishing line on top of the rod since this type of fishing rod is held with the guides and reel on top of the rod.

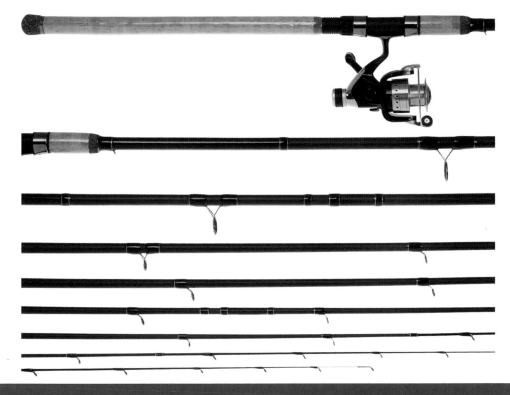

A fishing rod and reel is broken up visually here. The way a rod is constructed and tapered affects its action, or the amount it bends.

FISHING REELS

With a fiberglass or graphite fishing rod, you will need a fishing reel. A fishing reel can be found in the store where you find your fishing rod. Fishing reels come in different styles, types, and sizes.

One type of fishing reel is a spinning reel. This type of reel is used for casting lures and baits out at a distance from where you are. The spinning reel is simple to use and can be used in both freshwater and saltwater fishing. The advantage of a spinning reel is that you can cast whatever you are using to catch fish out to where the fish may be with little effort. The spinning reel will be underneath the fishing rod when the fishing rod is being held.

Another type of reel is a conventional reel. This type of reel can also be used for casting, but it is usually used on a conventional fishing rod, which is used for fishing with bait and some lures. When using a conventional fishing rod and reel, if the rod is being

A fisherman uses a spinning fishing reel to reel in a catch. Note how the reel lies beneath the rod in this kind of fishing.

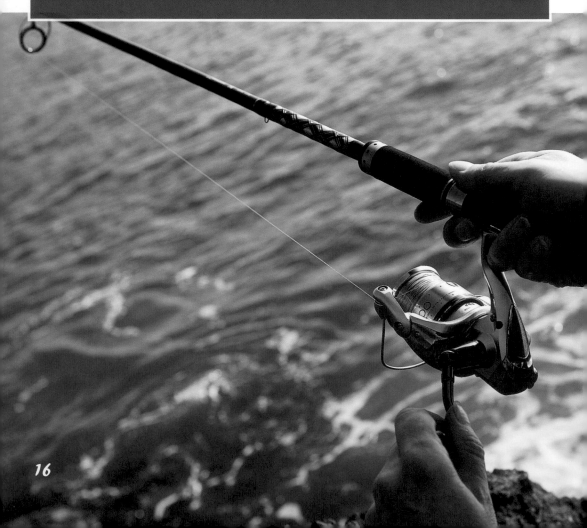

held by the fisherman, the reel will be on top of the fishing rod, not underneath as a spinning reel would be.

Both of these types of reels are sold in fishing supply store, tackle shops, or sporting goods stores. If you have any questions about these fishing reels at any of these locations, ask an employee; he or she will assist you and guide you to what you are looking for.

FISHING LINE

If you are fishing with a bamboo pole or wooden stick, you do not need a fishing reel; all you need is fishing line. Fishing line can be found in your local fishing supply store. If you are using a fiber-glass or graphite rod, fishing line is used on your reel and is the connection from your fishing rod and reel to the hook and bait.

There are all different sizes and colors of fishing line. Usually, the smaller the

Much like thread, fishing line is wrapped around and sold on a spool, which unspools on the fisherman's reel.

fish, the lighter the fishing line, and vice versa. The most common type is monofilament, which is almost transparent and hard for fish to see underwater. You can buy monofilament fishing line with different line strengths, meaning if the line has a 10-pound (4.5 kilogram) test rating, in theory the line will break when 10 pounds of pressure is put onto it. The pound test rating can range from a one-pound test to a 400-pound (181.4 kg) test.

The other type of fishing line is a braided fishing line. Braided fishing line is made from small fibers braided together to make one solid fishing line. It is stronger and thinner than monofilament, and, unlike the monofilament, the braided fishing line will not stretch. Fishermen sometimes prefer it because it is more sensitive and it is easier to tell when a fish hits the bait.

Be very careful using braided fishing line; it is very strong and jagged. If you let it rub against your bare flesh, it can easily cut you when it unspools quickly. Another one of its drawbacks is that it is more visible in water than monofilament. It can also be tougher on your gear and is recommended more for higher-end titanium or metal components.

TERMINAL TACKLE: HOOKS, SINKERS, AND FLOATS

You will now need hooks, swivels, sinkers, and floats to attach to the end of your line. These items are called terminal tackle. The hook is attached to the very end of your fishing line, and hooks come in many shapes and sizes. The type of hook you use depends on the type of fish and the type of bait.

TACKLE FOR SALTWATER FISHING

Fishing tackle for saltwater fishing is very similar to that used for freshwater fishing. The one big difference is size. Bigger rods, reels, and floats, and heavier sinks are usually needed, along with stronger line.

Of course, it all depends on what kind of fish you are hoping to reel in. Big tuna, shark, and other large fish require bigger gear. For bottom fish, you will probably use tackle comparable to that used for freshwater fishing.

Maintaining and replacing the equipment you have is also slightly different in saltwater environments. If using monofilament, replace it often, especially if it starts to look rough or feel dull. Rinse lures properly and soak reels in fresh water for a few hours before packing them away after trips. Salt water can really degrade your gear if you do not take care of it.

Floats, sinkers, hooks, rods, and reels are used in both saltwater and freshwater fishing.

As you move from the hook back along your line to your fishing rod, you may attach a sinker. A sinker is a piece of metal, usually lead, that is attached to your fishing line to sink the hook and bait to the bottom of the water. Sinkers, like hooks, come in different sizes with weights ranging from less than an ounce to over a pound. The weight of the sinker you use depends on the fishing conditions. In deep or fast-moving water, you will use a heavier sinker. For shallow or still water, you may choose only a very light weight or none at all.

If you want to keep your bait off the bottom of the water, you will use a float; if you want your bait on the bottom of the water, you will use only a sinker. Floats, like everything else we have discussed, come in different shapes and sizes. If you are fishing with heavy bait or in rough water, you may want to use a float that is bigger than normal. When using light bait or fishing in calm waters, your float may not have to be so big. Floats are used not only to keep your bait off the bottom but also as strike indicators. If a fish hits your bait, the float will move in a funny way or slip under the water, telling you that you have a fish.

LIFELIKE LURES

Instead of using bait to catch fish, you can use a fake bait, or a lure. Lures are made to resemble most bait fish, worms, frogs, insects, or other tempting delicacies that appeal to fish. A lure is usually cast out and retrieved by the fisherman. While being retrieved, the lure will resemble an injured bait fish or other source of food and, hopefully, the fish will think that it is real.

Fishing lures come in thousands of colors, shapes, sizes, and materials. Lures are used in all types of fishing, from fishing for small trout in streams to trying to catch that 1,000-pound (454 kg) marlin in the deep ocean. For any given situation, some lures will work better than others. That is why there are so many lures to choose from.

The best advice to follow when choosing a lure is to buy the lure that the person in the fishing store suggests you buy. The employee or manager at the store will probably know better than anyone which lures will catch the most fish because customers have probably been reporting back on which kinds have been working on the local fish and which have not.

CHAPTER 3

FISHING IN FRESHWATER

Those starting out in the sport of fishing will likely try fresh-water fishing first. Many North Americans have access to the wonderful coastal regions, but the majority of people are closer to freshwater fishing spots, like streams, creeks, rivers, and lakes. Most people reside too far from the coast to saltwater fish very often.

HOW CAN I TELL IF A BODY OF WATER IS FRESHWATER?

There are a few simple ways to tell if the water you are about to fish in is freshwater and not salt water. If you see that the body of water is surrounded by land, most likely the water is freshwater. You can even taste the water to make sure it doesn't taste salty, if there is any doubt. Before going out, look online or check a map of the area.

Generally, inland lakes and other water bodies are freshwater.

Your best fishing option may be a lake or pond close to your home. The first thing you should investigate is the cleanliness of the water. If you can see to the bottom, chances are the water is clean enough to hold fish.

Second, look for plants or weeds growing in the water. If you do not see any, the water is probably poisoned or polluted and won't have fish, either.

Last, look for signs of animal life, such as frogs, small fish, or turtles. If you see any in the water, chances are good there will be bigger fish, too.

A fly fisherman casts his line on the Margaree River on Cape Breton Island, in Nova Scotia, Canada. The river is well known for trout and especially Atlantic salmon, which spawn there.

WHAT KINDS OF FISH LIVE IN FRESHWATER?

Freshwater fish spend most or all of their lives in water that has usually no more than .05 percent salinity. Ocean water has a salinity of about 3.5 percent. There are many different kinds of freshwater fish that you can catch in your local fishing spot.

BASS

One of the most common kinds of freshwater fish is the largemouth bass. This fish lives in every state in the continental United States. It can live in small ponds, lakes, and even manmade reservoirs. The biggest largemouth bass caught on a rod and reel to date is 22 pounds, 4 ounces (10.09 kg).

In the southern parts of the United States, largemouth bass are fished all year round. In the northern states like New York and Michigan, largemouth bass can also be caught all year round, but they are easier to catch from April to October.

Largemouth bass are predators. They will feed on almost anything: small fish, frogs, mice, worms, crawfish, and similar critters. To locate these fish, find a fallen tree, weeds, or rocks in the water you are fishing; these places are popular spots for bass to congregate.

Another type of bass is the smallmouth bass. The smallmouth bass is a more active and smaller bass. The largest smallmouth bass ever caught was about 11 pounds (5 kg). The smallmouth bass is a member of the sunfish family and can be found in all states east of the Rocky Mountains except the states bordering the Gulf Coast. The smallmouth bass lives in clear, deep, rocky, cold water or in the rapid waters of streams and rivers.

Smallmouth bass are predators, just like their cousin the largemouth bass. Smallmouth bass feed on the same small animals as the largemouth bass, but they like bait that is smaller. To catch smallmouth bass, fishermen should use bait such as small minnows, worms, crawfish, and some small bugs.

PIKE

The pike family is another group of fish found in North America. The most prevalent type of fish in this group is the muskellunge, or the muskie. Muskies can be found in southern Canada and throughout Wisconsin, Michigan, Minnesota, Ohio, and New York; in the Susquehanna, Potomac, and Delaware river systems; and as far south as some of the waters in the Tennessee valley states. Muskies live in the clear, cool water of lakes, rivers, and flowages. The biggest muskie ever caught weighed 69 pounds, 15 ounces (about 30.4 kg). Muskies feed on larger bait fish such as small trout, bass, or larger shiners.

The northern pike can be found in most of Canada and many areas of the northern United States as far west as the Continental Divide. Pike feed all year long. They are less active in the winter months and more active in warm, springtime water. Pike are like bass in that they live and feed around structures such as weeds, fallen trees, and rocks. Pike feed in daylight, mostly on smaller fish. Early morning is a good time to catch them because that is when they are hungriest.

Another type of fish in the pike family is the pickerel. The pickerel is the smallest member of the pike family; 8- or 9-pound (3.6 to 4.8 kg) pickerel are the largest. Pickerel live in streams, lakes, and ponds in New England, New Jersey, and southern New York State. Pickerel feed on the same small fish as the northern pike.

THE PANFISH

The smallest group of fish are the panfish. Panfish consist of bluegills, crappies, rock bass, sunfish, and yellow perch. Panfish are mostly caught for food, and they can be found throughout the United States.

The key to catching panfish is to use small bait and to fish them very slowly. Worms—both red worms and mealworms—are the best bait. The bluegill, also called bream or brim, swims in schools, and the bigger ones can be found around their nests in warmer, shallower waters. Their nests consist of clean gravel and sandy beds, and they are easily seen.

Crappies are members of the sunfish family. Crappies can be found and caught in the same areas as the bluegill: in deep cover such as brush piles, docks, submerged or fallen trees, rock piles, and boulders. Crappies love to feed on small minnows. The biggest crappie ever caught was 5.2 pounds (2.4 kg).

Rock bass are also called the goggle eye or red eye. The biggest of the rock bass is about 12 inches (30.5 centimeters) long. Rock bass live in the same areas as the smallmouth bass. This small fish will take almost any small food including but not limited to worms, crawfish, minnows, grasshoppers, and other insects and grubs. The

Panfish get their name because they usually fit in the frying pans used to cook them. Some fishermen use the term for any small fish. This particular one is a freshwater sunfish.

best time to catch these fish is in the evening and at night.

Sunfish are probably the best known of the panfish. They are also called pumpkinseed. They have very small mouths, so small baits must be used. Sunfish live in the same waters as the bluegill. Because sunfish are easy to catch, they are a lot of fun for children.

Yellow perch are fun to catch. The biggest on record was approximately 4 pounds (1.81 kg). Yellow perch are found mostly in lakes and ponds. They will eat almost any live bait you put in front of them, and they are daytime feeders. Small minnows will be your best bait since the yellow perch will feed most aggressively on them. Yellow perch can also be caught on small lures.

THE IMITATION GAME: FLY-FISHING

The bait that fly fishers tie to the end of their rods is designed to imitate the live food of game fish. Game fish feed on insects, minnows, and other living prey in their environments. Fly-fishing can be done in either freshwater or salt water. Fly-fishing is immensely popular throughout North America and worldwide.

Fishing tackle used in fly-fishing is shown here, including a wide variety of lifelike lures.

Fly-fishing dates to the first or second centuries BCE in Macedonia, where brown trout anglers attached feathers to their hooks to imitate the insects in running streams. The materials used today include fur, feathers, thread, tinsel, and wool.

There is a special art and skill required in casting a fly. This is done in a way that to fish the fly will appear as if it is prey: an insect emerging from the stream, returning to it to lay eggs, or rising to the surface to split its outer skin and emerge with wings. Fly fishers may spend years perfecting their skills. It is an excellent way to hone athletic skill, it and helps one learn how to move with ease and grace.

TROUT

The final group of freshwater fish is trout: brook trout, brown trout, and rainbow trout. The brook trout is found mostly in small streams, but these fish also live in cold water and are found in ponds, lakes, and rivers. The biggest brook trout ever caught was 14 pounds, 8 ounces (6.6 kg). Brook trout can be found in most cold regions of the United States, particularly in the northeastern states. These fish feed on shrimp, crawfish, and some other small organisms. They can also be caught with worms and small bugs. When fishing for them, you can also use small lures, such as spinners and flies.

The brown trout originated in England. It averages about 10

pounds (4.5 kg) in the United States. Large brown trout will eat almost anything, including birds, frogs, and mice, but the brown trout's main diet consists of insects. Brown trout, also called sea trout, travel to the oceans, where freshwater mixes with salt water.

The rainbow trout is considered one of the greatest game fish of the world. The rainbow trout that return from the sea are called steelheads. Rainbow trout are also jumpers; when they are hooked, they put on a great display of aerial acrobatics. These trout like fast-moving streams. Like the other trout, rainbow trout feed on insects, but during some seasons of the year they will feed on larger bait, such as small fish, crawfish, or even freshwater shrimp.

A trout swims the depths at a nature center. Closely related to salmon, trout are one of the most popular game fish.

CATCHING EDIBLE FISH

All of the fish described here are edible. This means you can eat them safely. However, some fish may taste better than others. You also have to be careful of the small bones of the fish. When you catch a fish to bring home for dinner, give it to an adult to be properly cleaned, or filleted. As you gain experience, you will learn to fillet a fish properly yourself. Still, when you fillet and eat panfish or trout, which have been known to have a lot of small bones, it's often hard to clean out every little bone. Be careful and eat slowly so that you don't harm yourself.

CHAPTER 4

FISHING IN SALT WATER

About 72 percent of the Earth's surface is covered in water. Salt water makes up most of that—as much as 97 percent! It makes up the oceans, as well as the seas, most of which connect to them. You can taste the salt in seawater and even extract it. Take a container (or a plate or Frisbee, for example) and put ocean water in it. Leave it in the sun for some time. The water will evaporate and leave salt behind.

Much of the oceans are fished, though mostly by commercial fishermen. But many fishermen own or rent boats for their own fishing trips, while others can fish in salt water from the coast.

FISHING LOCATIONS

Besides the coast itself, salt water goes farther inland on bays and inlets. If you live in a state that borders the Atlantic or Pacific ocean

Fishing from the beach can be an enjoyable experience—even by yourself—and more economical and safer than fishing from a boat.

or the Gulf of Mexico, it is likely you live within driving distance of some great fishing.

All of the following saltwater types of fishing spots are productive, meaning they are places where you can catch a lot of fish—maybe even a very big fish—if you are in the right place at the right time.

PIERS, JETTIES, AND BRIDGES

If you want to do some saltwater fishing near your home and you or your family do not have a boat or a house near a beach or bay, there are some structures you can fish from.

A pier: A large wooden structure built into a harbor or other body of water and designed so that people can walk and stand above deeper water than they can get to from the shore alone.

A jetty: a structure of rocks or other building materials that usually juts out from a beach and that is usually home to a lot of different fish.

A bridge: any structure that crosses over water. Bridges inland are used for freshwater fishing. A bridge that connects one piece of land to another in a coastal area is a great spot to set up for fishing.

All of these structures can be fished from with ease. The main concern you should have is for your safety. When fishing from a man-made structure that juts out into or out over the bay or ocean, be especially careful. Stand clear of unprotected edges and never lean over a protective rail or rope. If you fall a great height onto water, even if it is deep enough, hitting the water can injure you or put you into shock, and you can then drown, even if you know how to swim. You can injure yourself on rocks or the ocean

Dock fishing is relaxing and convenient, and it often allows you to fish over deeper waters and cast even farther into a body of water than is possible from a beach or other shore.

floor. In addition, strong waves can drag you down or smash you against them or other objects.

FISHING FROM A BOAT

If you do not have a bridge, pier, or jetty to fish off of near your home, you may live near a marina that is home to public fishing boats or party boats. These boats are often for hire, meaning you pay a small fee to fish on them. These boats will supply you with rods, reels, and bait. You will be fishing with a lot of other people on this kind of boat and it could be crowded, but you have an opportunity to catch some nice fish. A boat can take you far enough that there are plenty of fish for everyone.

If you do not want to fish on a crowded boat, you can fish from a charter boat. These boats are usually smaller and much more expensive to use. However, you can fish with whomever you choose or by yourself, and the captain and first mate will usually fish for whatever catch you want. A party boat is limited, too, in the type of fish it allows or encourages customers to catch depending on the time of year. For example, a boat might go out for fluke during the spring and summer months, sea bass and porgy in the fall, and blackfish in the winter. These guidelines, naturally, vary for the different coastal fishing regions all over the United States and Canada.

Boat fishing may restrict you to rules that determine which fish are catchable. Despite what you may see others do, always make sure to wear a lifejacket on board.

SURF CASTING: SURFING FROM THE BEACH

The beach is the next place you can look to fish from if you do not have access to a boat or dock. Even though your chances are better from structures that give you better water access, many big fish are caught right in the surf just off the beach.

WHAT ARE SOME TYPES OF SALTWATER FISH?

There are thousands of different types of saltwater fish around the world. What follows are descriptions of the more popular fish groups.

MARLIN

One type of saltwater fish is the marlin. The marlin is one of the most popular game fish in the world. Marlins are not considered very flavorful, so they are caught not so much for food as for the challenge—they put up a tremendous fight and make dramatic jumps when they are hooked.

There are a few types of marlin. From the largest to the smallest, they are the black marlin, blue marlin, striped marlin, and white marlin. The marlin has a bill on the front of its body. As a result, it is sometimes called a billfish. Marlins feed on very large bait, such as tuna, mahimahi (dolphinfish), and jacks.

The marlin is not the only game fish that has a bill. Other fish that have bills and are chased by fishermen are the sailfish, which is a tremendous jumper; the swordfish, which chefs and food fans consider the tastiest of the billfish (and the strongest, pound for pound); and the spearfish, which has the shortest bill.

TUNA

Tuna are chased for food rather than for their fight (that is, the fight fish put up rather than be caught), but they are among the toughest fish of the oceans when it comes to allowing themselves to be

This Atlantic bluefin tuna feeds in the waters of the Gulf of Saint Lawrence, a body of water feeding into the Atlantic Ocean adjacent to Canada's east coast.

reeled in. Tuna are found all over the world in both cold and warm waters. There are several different types of tuna. From the largest to the smallest, they are:

- The bluefin tuna, which can grow to over one thousand pounds
- The bigeye tuna, which is flavorful and hence a major type of fish used for sushi, both in Japan and worldwide
- The yellowfin tuna, which is also very flavorful
- The longfin albacore, the type of tuna usually canned for sale in grocery stores and supermarkets
- The blackfin tuna, which is mostly found in the warmer ocean areas of the world

There are a few types of tuna that are less sought after, due to being considered not as tasty. These tuna are the skipjack tuna, false albacore, green bonito, and Atlantic bonito, and thry are all significantly smaller than the rest. Tuna usually roam the deep parts of the oceans searching for large schools of squid, mackerel, herring, and other small fish. They can be caught by trolling, which means to pull either lures or fresh bait at a fixed speed behind the boat from which you are fishing.

SHARKS

Sharks are still hunted for sport throughout the world. The most popular sharks to catch are the great white shark, which is the largest of the predator sharks and the most feared; the mako shark, which is the shark most targeted for its great fight; the thresher shark, which has the longest tail of all sharks; the tiger shark, which is probably the most deadly of the sharks; and the hammerhead shark, which is the most ferocious and most feared by divers and swimmers because it is known to roam shallow waters. There are too many sharks to name, but these sharks are the most popular among fishermen. Some other sharks sometimes targeted by fishermen are the blacktip shark, bull shark, blue shark, reef shark, brown shark, and dusky shark.

All of these sharks give a dramatic fight when hooked, but they should not be killed just for that. Most of them are inedible; so if you do catch a shark someday, let it go if you do not plan to eat it. This should probably be your policy for any species of fish. Because of overhunting, many species of sharks are now protected and others are restricted in the numbers that can be fished in any given season or year. The more people learn about how harmful shark overfishing has been, and the more respect people gain for sharks' very crucial roles in the food chain, the less people will hopefully choose to hunt shark.

BOTTOM FISH

Bottom fish are the fish that roam the bottom of the sea. They are often found near sunken or submerged objects, including ships, rock piles, or ledges. The following are some of the most popular with fishermen: the blackfish, which is good to eat and can be found around sunken structures and formations in colder waters; the sea bass, which is edible and is very abundant around structures and sometimes in open bottom; the flounder, which is found in muddy bottom and feeds on small organisms; the summer flounder, which looks similar to the flounder but is more aggressive and feeds on

SHARK ATTACK!

Don't worry—chances are you won't be attacked by a shark. Worldwide, there are only about three hundred documented cases of shark attacks each year. The great white shark attacks generally because it confuses humans with its usual food, seals and sea lions. The bull shark, on the other hand, will attack a human for no reason.

Although the odds of your being attacked by a shark are remote—while swimming or diving, you are one thousand times more likely to drown than to be attacked by a shark— it is wise to take precautions.

The great white shark is among the largest and most important predators in the earth's oceans. Despite the shark's fearsome appearance and ferocity, great whites very rarely attack humans.

- **Don't swim or dive in areas where sharks are common. Thus, avoid swimming at dusk or after dark. (This is when sharks feed and swim closer to shore.)**
- **Always swim with others and never alone.**
- **Don't go in the water where others are fishing.**
- **Do not enter the water if you see large numbers of fish or if fish are acting strangely.**

small fish, shrimp, and crabs; and the cod, which roams the bottom of the ocean looking for wrecks. There are a tremendous number of bottom fish all over the world. The more popular ones live in the northeastern waters of the Atlantic Ocean.

STRIPED BASS

The striped bass is a fantastic game fish. It is challenging to catch, and most fishermen will do almost anything to catch one of these trophy fish, no matter what their size. The striped bass got its name because of the stripes that run down the side of its body. This fish feeds on most bottom-dwelling fish, including the ones mentioned above. It also feeds on eels, bunker, herring, and some types of crab. The striped bass can be caught with lures, live bait, and even some dead cut bait (pieces of dead fish used as bait).

The largest striped bass weigh 50 pounds (22.7 kg) or more. People catch striped bass from boats, the beach, piers, jetties, and docks, and even from the tops of bridges. If you are ever able to catch one of these great game fish, you should be proud of your accomplishment.

BLUEFISH

The bluefish, like the striped bass, feeds on most of the smaller fish that cross its path. It derives its name from its blue back. Bluefish are very aggressive fish, and they are doubly dangerous due to their extremely sharp teeth. With these, they can cut through another fish like a knife through butter. Bluefish are not considered much of a delicacy because their meat tends to be a little oily.

Bluefish can be caught on almost anything you put at the end of your fishing rod if they are in a feeding frenzy. In the northeastern part of the United States, bluefish are often very abundant and can be seen feeding on the surface of bays and the ocean. Small baby bluefish are called snappers, and when the water gets warm, they can be caught off most beaches, piers, and docks.

WEAKFISH

The weakfish gets its name because of its weak jaw. When hooked, the mouth of the weakfish has a tendency to tear if too much pressure is put on it. Weakfish feed on all of the same fish as bluefish and striped bass, but they can sometimes be more aggressive than bluefish and bass. At other times, they are not aggressive at all. Weakfish like the same living conditions as bluefish and striped bass, which is warm water and areas with a lot of bait. The weakfish is also called the sea trout because it can have a color pattern similar to that of its cousin, the freshwater brown trout.

Small baby bluefish (snapper) are shown in a bucket. Their small size—fitting in a person's palm—should not fool you. They do bite, especially in late summer, when they feed voraciously.

OTHER FISH THAT LIVE IN SALT WATER

There are other saltwater fish you will likely encounter, especially off the coast of the northeastern United States. One bottom fish that is small and edible is the kingfish. The sea robin is a bottom-feeding fish with large pectoral fins that resemble a bird's wings in flight in the water, hence its name. There is also the porgy, which exists close to the bottom of the ocean. One unusual saltwater fish, the pufferfish, or blowfish, is known for the way it puffs up to resemble a ball in the water. But it is also known for its poison, which makes it one of the most dangerous fish to eat. In Japan, where it is called *fugu*, and other cultures, its nontoxic parts are separated and prepared as a delicacy. Overall, the world's oceans and seas provide a nearly limitless variety of fishing opportunities.

CHAPTER 5

FISHING TODAY: CONTROVERSIES, CRISIS, AND THE FUTURE

Well into the twenty-first century, the fishing public and commercial fishing industry are embroiled in controversy over fishing rights and responsibilities. Who has the right to catch which species, in what amounts, and in which regions of the world? Commercial fishing interests are at odds with recreational fishermen (sportsmen or hobbyists), while governments and environmental groups and many concerned citizens are sometimes at odds with the fishing industry.

OVERFISHING

Overfishing by both commercial and recreational fishermen has caused a drop-off in numbers of fish around the world. Most scientists who study the weather and environment also say that other human activities, such as direct pollution of the ocean, and indirect causes, such as the burning of fossil fuels, are seriously threatening fish stocks everywhere. As a result, there have been ever more restrictions on fishing for certain species, both by individual nations themselves and by the international community. It is often tough to enforce many of these rules, especially because people can make a lot of money by breaking them.

Recreational fishermen tend to believe that commercial fishing depletes the amount of fish in the ocean. Commercial fishermen tend to believe that they have every right to fish for any species they choose. When it comes to regulating who can fish for a specific species, the two often disagree.

This commercial fishing boat—sometimes called a trawler or dragger—brings its haul of winter (black back) flounder, lobster, and cod to port in Gloucester, Massachusetts.

Governments try to work out compromises to keep both groups happy. They do this by giving each group of fishermen rights to certain fish species and certain fishing grounds.

TERRITORIAL RIGHTS

Problems arise when nations disagree on which country has the right to fish specific areas of the oceans. Each country has possession of the 200 miles (322 kilometers) of ocean along its coastlines. Each country regulates the fishing that goes on within those areas. When a country fishes in another country's waters without that country's permission, legal issues regarding who can fish where arise. These are sometimes resolved through international courts and treaties, but there are still many ocean regions in dispute worldwide.

FISHING REGULATIONS

State and federal governments have laws regulating fishing and the size of fish that can be kept by both commercial and recreational fishermen. These laws prevent the depletion of certain fish species. These laws are enforced by local, state, and federal law enforcement. This can mean enforcement agencies boarding boats or meeting boats at their docks and checking the size and amount of fish the fishermen have caught. Fisherman violating these rules are fined.

Every year the laws change. You can find copies of them at fishing retail locations and at offices and ranger stations at national parks and forests. Every state has a fish and wildlife commission or regulatory agency, and they have these rules available online, too. These websites also provide instructions on how to obtain proper fishing licenses and other credentials, if these are required.

AQUACULTURE: INDUSTRIAL FISHERIES

To make up for overfishing in the wild, businesses are raising fish in very large fish tanks or enclosures separated from the rest of the ocean by a net. Raising fish this way is called aquaculture. Aquaculture takes pressure off the world's migrating fish stocks. Without

This aquaculture farm at the University of Arizona Environmental Research Laboratory in Tucson, Arizona, helps preserve and expand fish stocks.

such pressure on certain fish species, it is hoped that those species are able to recover their numbers. Maybe in the future they will no longer be considered a depleted fish stock. There are specific types of fish that are raised in tanks to be sold in fish markets. Those fish include the catfish, striped bass, salmon, and trout.

THE COMPETITION: FISHING TOURNAMENTS

Have you ever watched television and seen a fishing show? Maybe you enjoy watching fishing competitions or instructional fishing videos online, via YouTube or other video-sharing platforms. In many cases, the host of the fishing show or the person who posts the video is a professional fisherman. A professional fisherman is a person who fishes in fishing tournaments, sometimes for big cash prizes. Usually, these tournaments are won by the fishermen who catch the biggest fish. For many fishermen, the bragging rights of getting the biggest catch even outweigh the cash prize.

There are many different types of fishing tournaments held throughout the world. Sometimes the first prize in a fishing tournament can be as much as $300,000. Largemouth bass fishing tournaments are probably the most popular type of fishing tournament in the United States today. In a largemouth bass tournament, a professional fisherman and an amateur fisherman usually fish together on the same boat. The professional fisherman is limited to five fish, and the goal for each fisherman is to catch the biggest five fish he or she can by the end of the day. This goes on for two or three days. At the end of the tournament, the fisherman with the fish that, when taken all together, weigh the most wins the tournament and takes the prize money.

There are also marlin tournaments. Large sport fishing boats with about four or five fishermen on board go out and try to catch the biggest marlin. These last at least two days, and sometimes the

FIGHTING FOR A SUSTAINABLE SPORT

While it is estimated that sport fishing makes up less than 12 percent of the global fish harvest every year, sport fishermen have embraced sustainability and environmental preservation. They realize catching all the fish they can or harming their habitat will destroy the sport sooner rather than later. Some effort now will prevent long-term decline and disaster.

Kirk Deeter, an editor at *Field & Stream* magazine, says that fighting for clean water has to be part of any larger solution. Using fly-fishing as an example, the number one threat to the sport is "shrinking access to opportunity . . . It's about having a place to go, or lack thereof . . . We need rivers, streams, lakes, and ponds with cool, clean water."

Rules are also important, even if they sometimes seem arbitrary or random—for example, seasonal limits on catches. These balance fish habitats and anglers' needs. In some parts of the world, such as in the United Kingdom, fish poaching is a big problem. Luckily, most American and Canadian fishing enthusiasts follow the rules. In addition, proper licensing and permits help pay for everyone to enjoy fishing for a long time to come.

winning fish can weigh up to 1,000 pounds (454 kg).

Other types of tournaments are local fishing tournaments for local fish. These tournaments are not as popular as the other tournaments we have discussed because they pay out much smaller prizes. Besides cash prizes, local contests help people meet other fishing hobbyists and swap advice and stories.

The drawback with these fishing tournaments is the often unfortunate and unnecessary killing of fish. The goal of every fisherman in these tournaments is to catch the biggest fish. Since they don't know if they have the biggest fish until they get back to the

A teenager poses with a salmon. Attitudes are slowly changing to embrace the idea that those who fish should try to minimize harm to fish through humane catch-and-release practices.

dock, they have a tendency to kill most of the big fish that they catch. You should take this into consideration before you decide to participate in a tournament.

CATCH AND RELEASE (THE ETHICAL WAY)

Some fishermen and fishing groups have made an effort in recent years to encourage more ethical fishing practices. Many species of fish have about a one-in-three chance of dying when they are caught and thrown back, depending on how they are handled. A few measures can help alleviate this needless loss.

One measure is to use barbless circle hooks. There is some proof that there is very little difference in how well each kind of hook helps catch fish. But barbless ones can reduce the chance that fish will get injured by being gut-hooked. Removing a hook using needle-nose pliers instead of just tearing it out will prevent unnecessary suffering and injury to fish. Decide quickly, too, whether you want to keep a fish or not because the longer a fish is out of water, the more chance it will be permanently injured by its inability to breathe.

Holding fish horizontally—like they exist underwater—is also key to making sure the internal organs are not injured by the weight of the innards. Only hold fish vertically that you plan to eat (when photographing a catch, for example). Keeping your hands wet when you handle a fish will help it keep its protective, wet coating.

It is up to the current generation to make sure that fishing—as a pastime, hobby, business, sport, and even way of life—remains viable for all future generations.

GLOSSARY

AMATEUR A person who participates in a sport primarily for pleasure, rather than for professional or financial reasons. Amateurs do not fish to make a living or as professional sportspeople.

BILL The part of a marlin, sailfish, or swordfish that sticks out from its face. These fish use their bills to hurt the fish they are going to eat.

CATCH AND RELEASE The practice of letting fish go when a fisherman plans not to eat them.

CONVENTIONAL Describes a fishing rod or reel that is not a spinning reel or fly reel.

DEAD CUT Bait chunks of dead fish that are put on a fishing hook to catch other fish.

DELICACY A choice or expensive food.

FLARE Device that lights up so brightly that people can see it from very long distances. Flares are used to tell other people that you need help.

GRIP The part of the fishing rod that you hold on to.

GRUB A small insect used for bait; it is the larval stage, or first life stage, of a beetle.

GUIDE The part of the fishing rod that the line is put through so it can go from the reel to the tip of the rod.

HERRING A small bait fish that roams the colder waters of oceans and bays. Larger fish often feed on herring.

JETTY A line of large rocks that extends into a sea, lake, or river to protect the shore from erosion.

LEDGE An underwater ridge or reef, especially near the shore.

LIFE PRESERVER A device that floats that you put on like a jacket to keep from drowning.

LIVE BAIT Live fish put on a hook and then back into the water to catch bigger fish.

MONOFILAMENT An opaque material that is used to make a fishing line.

PIER A wooden structure that is built out over the water so people can fish more easily and in deeper water.

PREDATOR An animal that hunts and consumes other animals for food.

REEL SEAT The part of a fishing rod where the fishing reel is attached and tightened so that it does not fall off the rod.

RESERVOIR A body of water, made by man, where water is stored for irrigation or drinking.

SHANK The long part of a fish hook that acts like a backbone to the rest of the hook.

TERMINAL TACKLE The hooks, sinkers, floats, and lures that you put at the end of your fishing line.

TRAWLER Also known as a dragger, a fishing trawler is a kind of fishing boat that pulls large catches of fish all at once using nets cast into the ocean.

FOR MORE
INFORMATION

American Sportfishing Association
1001 North Fairfax Street, Suite 501
Alexandria VA 22314
(703) 519-9691
Website: http://asafishing.org
The American Sportfishing Association has grown from a trade organization for fishing tackle manufacturers since its founding in 1933 to
champion the entire sportfishing industry and movement.

Canadian Parks and Wilderness Society (CPWS)
880 Wellington Street, Suite 506
Ottawa, ON K1R 6K7
Canada
(800) 333-WILD (9453)
Website: http://www.cpaws.org
Since 1963, the Canadian Parks and Wilderness Society has been a
leader in wilderness protection, having helped preserve more than
two-thirds of Canada's current protected wild areas.

National Park Service (NPS)
1849 C Street NW
Washington, DC 20240
(202) 208-6843
Website: http://www.nps.gov
The National Park Service is the agency of the U.S. federal government
in charge of the nation's national parks, many of its national monu-
ments, and various historical and heritage properties.
Ontario Federation of Anglers and Hunters (OFAH)
4601 Guthrie Drive, P.O. Box 2800
Peterborough, ON K9J 8L5

Canada
(705) 748-6324
Website: https://www.ofah.org
The Ontario Federation of Anglers and Hunters is the province of Ontario's largest nonprofit fish and wildlife conservation organization, made up of individual hunters and fishermen, member clubs, and other enthusiasts.

Trout Unlimited
1777 N. Kent Street, Suite 100
Arlington, VA 22209
(800) 834-2419
(703) 522-0200
Website: http://www.tu.org
Trout Unlimited has existed for more than fifty years to promote fishing, conservation, stream restoration, fish restocking, and coordinating member and volunteer efforts for all of its activities and goals.

Sierra Club
85 Second Street, Second Floor
San Francisco, CA 94105
(415) 977-5500
Website: http://www.sierraclub.org
The Sierra Club is one of the largest nonprofit organizations in the Untied States and internationally that advocates for conservation and environmental protection. It also sponsors outdoor activities for all citizens.

WEBSITES

Because of the changing number of Internet links, Rosen Publishing has developed an online list of websites related to the subject of this book. This site is updated regularly. Please use this link to access this list:

http://www.rosenlinks.com/OUT/Fish

FOR FURTHER READING

Bagur, Daniel. *Where the Fish Are: A Science-Based Guide to Stalking Freshwater Fish*. New York, NY: Ragged Mountain Press/McGraw-Hill, 2009

Bockneck, Jonathan, and Charles Piddock. *World Fishing* (Global Issues). Calgary, Alberta, Canada: Weigl Educational Publishers Ltd., 2014.

Burlingame, Jeff. *How to Freshwater Fish Like a Pro* (Outdoor Sports Skills). New York, NY: Enslow Publishers, 2014.

Heos, Bridget. *Ice Fishing* (Fishing: Tips & Techniques). New York, NY: Rosen Publishing, 2012.

Paterson, Judy Monroe. *Fishing in Lakes and Ponds* (Fishing: Tips & Techniques). New York, NY: Rosen Publishing, 2012.

Payment, Simone. *Bass Fishing* (Fishing: Tips & Techniques). New York, NY: Rosen Publishing, 2012.

Price, Steve. *The Fish That Changed America: True Stories About the People Who Made Largemouth Bass Fishing an All-American Sport*. New York, NY: Skyhorse Publishing, 2014.

Sparano, Vin T. *Complete Guide to Fresh and Saltwater Fishing*. New York, NY: Universe Publishing, 2015.

Wolny, Philip. *Avoiding Danger on the Hunt* (Hunting: Pursuing Wild Game). New York, NY: Rosen Publishing, 2012.

Wolny, Philip. *Waterfowl* (Hunting: Pursuing Wild Game). New York, NY: Rosen Publishing, 2011.

INDEX

ABOUT THE AUTHOR

Philip Wolny is a writer and editor from Queens, New York. His other outdoors-related titles for Rosen Publishing include *Waterfowl* and *Avoiding Danger on the Hunt*.

Captain Dane Solomon started fishing when he was about two or three. His fishing knowledge comes from going out on the water and finding fish, reading books, and watching other, more experienced fishermen. He is a fishing charter captain and has produced his own television show, *Fishing Long Island*. He really loves to teach young people how to fish.

PHOTO CREDITS

Cover, p. 1 Dudarev Mikhail/Shuttersrock.com; p. 5 Loop Images/ Universal Images Group/Getty Images; p. 7 Nigel Pavitt/AWL Images/ Getty Images; pp. 10-11 bikeriderlondon/Shutterstock.com; p. 14 Civdis/Shutterstock.com; p. 15 Kovalchuk Oleksandr/Shutterstock. com; p. 16 Martin Leigh/Oxford Scientific/Getty Images; p. 17 © iStockphoto.com/PhotosbyAbby; p. 19 doug4537/E+/Getty Images; p. 23 Cindy Creighton/Shutterstock.com; p. 27 © iStockphoto.com/ Sasha Radosavljevic; p. 28 © iStockphoto.com/Fertnig; p. 30 Annette Shaff/Shutterstock.com; p. 33 Chris Bernard/E+/Getty Images; p. 35 Ron Levine/Digital Vision/Getty Images; p. 37 © iStockphoto.com/ martinedoucet; p. 39 Brian J. Skerry/National Geographic Magazines/ Getty Images; p. 42 Elsa Hoffman/Shutterstock.com; p. 45 Ira Block/ National Geographic Magazines/Getty Images; p. 48 Jeff Rotman/Pho-tolibrary/Getty Images; p. 50 Travel Images/UIG/Getty Images; p. 53 Grant Faint/The Image Bank/Getty Images; cover and interior pages Iwona Grodzka/iStock/Thinkstock (twig frame), AKIRA/amanaimag-esRF/Thinkstock (wood frame)

Photo Researcher: Philip Wolny